The Gift of Happiness
Belongs to Those
Who Unwrap It

The Gift of Happiness Belongs to Those Who Unwrap It

◆

and Other Tidbits for Living the Good Life
by One Smart Cookie

J.T. O'Hara

**Andrews McMeel
Publishing**

Kansas City

www.andrewsmcmeel.com

Library of Congress Cataloging-in-Publication Data

O'Hara, J.T., 1934–
    The gift of happiness belongs to those who unwrap it: and other tidbits for
    living the good life by One Smart Cookie / J.T. O'Hara.
        p. cm.
    ISBN 0-8362-6770-2
    1. Conduct of life—Quotations, maxims, etc. I. Title.
    BF637.C5039 1998
    170'.44—dc21   98-5939
                                                         CIP

Design by Tanya Maiboroda

ATTENTION: SCHOOLS AND BUSINESSES
Andrews McMeel books are available at quantity discounts with bulk purchase
for educational, business, or sales promotional use. For information, please write
to: Special Sales Department, Andrews McMeel Publishing, 4520 Main Street,
Kansas City, Missouri 64111.

To

Joe Rubinstein,

wherever you are!

◆

The Gift of Happiness
Belongs to Those
Who Unwrap It

When the heart speaks,
the mind turns to
peanut butter.

The only time success comes before work is in the dictionary.

Rather fail with honor than succeed by deceit.

If you think you can or think you can't you're right.

4

As Freud said, "Sometimes a cigar is just a cigar."

5

Before you give a person
a piece of your mind,
be sure you have
enough of it left.

6

If at first you don't succeed,
you're running about
average.

Concentrate on the
Major Few and ignore
the Trivial Many.

The wages of sin
are unreported.

9

When you don't talk, you hear yourself better.

If the grass is greener on the other side, maybe yours needs more watering.

11

12

One must always be discreet
in one's indiscretions.

A man is judged by the company he avoids.

13

People always speak the truth, but sometimes by the time they finish speaking it, it is no longer true.

14

Happiness is good health
and a bad memory.

Husbands are like
fires. They go out
if unattended.

Love and scandal are the best sweeteners of tea.

A perpetual vacation
is a good working definition
of hell.

You're never too old to have a happy childhood.

If you want to be happy

for an hour, get drunk.

If you want to be happy for

a weekend, get married.

If you want to be happy

forever, be a gardener.

In the world of computers,
never trust a man with
a floppy disc.

Be an optimist,
because tomorrow has
never happened.

A winner is always vitalized
and a loser is always
victimized.

24

Always stay away from emotionally handcuffed people.

A balloon rises not because of its color, but because of what's inside it.

25

A man who wants to lead
the orchestra must turn
his back on the crowd.

Everyone on the planet can be a billionaire; it's just that each one doesn't have the consciousness.

Your body moves on the path of your expectations.

Most good women are hidden treasures who are only safe because nobody looks for them.

30

The way to do is to be.

Love is letting your light
shine after your fuse
has blown.

32

Treat your friends as you do
your paintings; place them
in the best light.

It's hard to hear what a
bearded man is saying.
He can't speak above
a whisker.

You can't teach an old dogma new tricks.

God is too big to be squeezed into any religion.

To live a worthwhile life,
you should know early on
what you want written on
your tombstone.

A day of worry is more
exhausting than a
week of work.

Never invest in
anything that eats
or needs repair.

Don't worry if your
children never listen to you;
worry that they are always
watching you.

40

Words mean nothing;
the performance is everything.

If you pay people peanuts, you get monkeys.

42

To express your feelings
is risk.

When it comes to foreign food, the less authentic the better.

Before you can break out of prison, you must realize you're locked up.

Make your sense of justice a magnificent and endless obsession.

45

Before you say anything
about anyone, let your words
pass through three gates.
Is it kind? Is it true?
Is it necessary?

A bird in the hand
is dead.

The best things in life are free; it's the worst things that are expensive.

Love is unconditional
commitment to an
imperfect person.

49

Once a week, take a close
inventory of yourself and
your destiny.

Don't look back in anger.
Don't look forward in fear.
But look around you
in awareness.

Religion is for people who are afraid of going to hell. Spirituality is for people who have been there.

52

Improvise, adapt, overcome.

Remember, a kick in the ass
is a step forward.

In Hollywood, writers are considered only the first drafts of human beings.

Writing is turning blood into ink.

The world is a madhouse,
so it's only right that it is
patrolled by armed idiots.

Applause is the
only appreciated
interruption.

Aim high!
It's no harder
to shoot the feathers
off an eagle than to shoot
the fur off a skunk.

60

Only Catholics and rapists don't use birth control.

You teach best what you most need to know.

Think classy...
you'll be classy.

Love makes passion but
money makes marriage.

There are no perfect men—
only perfect intentions.

Use soft words and hard arguments.

Don't fall in love with love; otherwise, you'll drown in the complexities.

We all can't be beautiful.

We all can't be rich.

But we all can have

good manners.

When a boat is in rough
waters and it doesn't rock,
it breaks.

It is our deeds that
determine our fate;
how far we go, and not
the place from which
we begin.

Definition of Flu—
Feeling Lousy Under
these conditions.

Poor is the man
who depends on
other people's
permission.

Life hardly ever lives up
to our anxieties.

The Greeks say a friend is
a single soul dwelling
in two bodies.

When you hear, you listen.

When you say, you remember.

When you do, you learn.

Talent is a flame.
Genius is a fire.

Count your blessings.
Get high on endorphins.

Journalism is
history in a hurry.

Success is never final,

and failure is never fatal.

It's courage that counts.

Nothing is good or bad—thinking makes it so.

Fear is the
darkroom where
negatives are
developed.

Even a dumb steer knows
when he is grazing in the
wrong pasture.

82

The most exclusive resort in the world is home.

One must never be in a hurry to end a day; there are too few of them in a lifetime.

8 4

Don't fall until you see the
whites of their lies.

There is no future in any job.
The future lies in the man
who holds the job.

There are some things
more painful than the truth,
but I can't think of them.

Never retire.
Just work yourself
to death.

88

Chance makes brothers, hearts make friends.

Keep your mouth shut
when you're swimming and
when you're angry.

Love that is
not expressed is
not love at all.

Never engage in a battle of
wits with an unarmed person.

Traveling in the company
of those we love is
home in motion.

The three best
doctors are nature,
time, and patience.

To handle yourself,
use your head.
To handle others,
use your heart.

Worry is the misuse of your imagination.

There is nothing that
one says that is unique.
It's the package that
is unique.

Things are so tough these days that hookers are living from hand to mouth.

Even a woodpecker owes his
success to his head.
He uses it.

If you fail
to prepare,
you're prepared
to fail.

The road to success
is paved with elbow grease
and perspiration.
Maybe that's why it's
so slippery.

Bloom where you
are planted!

If two people who love each
other let a single instant
wedge itself between
them, it grows.
It becomes a month, a year,
a century... it becomes
too late.

Better to have an inch of dog
than miles of pedigree.

104

Scared money never wins.

True affluence is
not needing anything.

Character consists
of what you do on the
third and fourth try.

Experience is what you get
when you don't get
what you want.

Despair is a narcotic.
It lulls the mind into
indifference.

When making
dinner for a friend,
don't forget the
kisses.

Hollywood is where they place you under contract, instead of under observation.

Progress
always involves risks.
You can't steal
second base and keep
your foot on first.

Whatever your lot in life is, build on it.

Don't try to shovel sand
against the tide.

Suffering is always optional.

The gift of
happiness belongs
to those who
unwrap it.

When a person whom
one loves is in the world alive
and well, then to miss them
is only a *new* sharpness
in experience.

We must give up last night
in order for us to be
ready for tonight.

118

Blessed are the flexible,
for they shall not be bent
out of shape.

Of course, there must be
subtleties in living.
Just make sure you make
them obvious.

119

120

If you close one eye, you have to blink the rest of your life.

Think twice. Do once.

Remember, the
reason for doing the
right thing today
is tomorrow.

If you know how to swim,
you can change horses
in midstream.

124

Those who sail without oars
have a better chance
with the wind.

When you're going through
hell, don't stop and
take pictures.

When elephants fight, it is the grass that suffers.

Travel light
and you can sing in
the robber's face.

128

If you always do
what you've always done,
you will always get what
you've always gotten.

Two prisoners were in jail. One saw the stars; the other, the bars. Which one are you?

129

130

Only love those who know how to love.

When you don't have red,
use blue.

Every style that is
not boring is a
good one.

A rolling football gathers no score.

133

134

Art is the elimination
of the unnecessary.

Watch the turtle;
he only makes progress when
he sticks his neck out.

When that which is perfect
is to come, that which is
imperfect shall come
to an end.

In the music business they say, "If you can't be grand, be upright."

Always practice
random kindness
and senseless acts
of beauty.

At sea we don't fight the wind, we learn how to use it.

It takes a woman
a long time to learn that
a flirtation is attention
without intention.

A turning point is life's
invitation to come up higher.

The pleasure seeker does not grow; he avoids pain.

No matter how much
cats fight, there always seem
to be plenty of kittens.

144

Your mind is your
thought factory.
Make sure not to produce
any toxic wastes.

A beached shark
doesn't hurt anyone.

The trouble with the
Me Generation is that they
worship the creation more
than the creator.

Don't confuse
your net worth with
your self-worth.

148

Feeling is healing.

Spain has her matadors;
the United States has
her politicians.

150

The morning is the rudder
of the day.

Anything that angers you, conquers you.

I never give them hell,
I just tell the truth and they
think it's hell.

Love looks with the mind,
not the eyes.

The only place the music
comes out is where the
needle touches.
The moment of contact
is what is creative.

Give a man a fish
and you feed him for a day.
Teach a man to fish
and you get rid of him
on weekends.

Common sense
is genius dressed in its
working clothes.

U.S. Navy regulations:

Stay alive.

Accomplish the mission.

Have some fun.

158

A naked woman aboard a ship calms the sea.

Schizophrenia beats
dining alone.

Being a mistress
means never having to say
you're tired.

Failure, not success,
is the teacher.

It is better to lose with
a smart person than to win
with a dumb one.

A good politician is as rare as
an honest burglar.

164

How do I love thee:
Let me clue thee in.

You can't make an omelet
without breaking a few eggs.

How come a six-year-old
whiskey can shake a
forty-year-old man?

You only know
what something
is worth when you
pay for it.

Remember, it's the high-stepping fillies that make the best mares.

A nun who walks in her sleep
is a Roman Catholic.

Unless you're the lead dog, your view never changes.

Only dead fish swim with the stream.

No wind is favorable to the sailor who doesn't know where he is going.

One person with belief is
worth more than ninety
without interest.

174

I was born in Brooklyn
because my mother wanted
me to be near her.

Trust in God,
but lock your car.

176

Poor people save money.

Rich people move it around.

Cats are like Baptists.
They raise hell but you can't
catch them at it.

Marriage is the
only war in which
you sleep with
the enemy.

If voting changed anything
in the country they'd
make it illegal.

The only time a woman can change a man is when he's a baby.

Hollywood's like granola.
Take away the fruits and nuts
and you've got cereal.

182

Flies spread disease—
keep yours zipped.

If you like peace and quiet,
get a phoneless cord.

184

Friends are the family
you have chosen.

A poacher who shoots
at a rabbit may scare
big game away.

Idle dreamers have given visionaries a bad name.

What really flatters a man
is that you think he is
worth flattering.

When the eagles are silent,
the parrots begin to jabber.

An ounce of mother
is worth a ton
of priest.

The most handicapped person in the world is a negative thinker.

Live your life like you have a terminal illness.

The cleverly expressed opposite of any generally accepted idea is worth a fortune to somebody.

One good friend is worth
ten lousy relatives.

A man is weak if he looks outside for help.

A coward is incapable
of exhibiting love—it is the
prerogative of the brave.

There is no way to weld
a broken promise.

If at first you don't succeed,
destroy all evidence that
you tried.

Stay away from hard liquor—
that's how the cucumber
became a pickle.

You might be too old
to cut the mustard,
but you're not too old
to lick the jar.

It's a dream until
you write it down—
then it's a goal.

We are shaped and fashioned
by what we love.

202

I'd love to be in heaven
ten minutes before the devil
discovers I'm dead.

Never get into fights with ugly people—they have nothing to lose.

204

If a man is sitting backward
on a horse, why do we assume
that he's going the
wrong way?

To be or not to be—
there is no try.

206

Creative minds
always survive
despite bad
training.

You are what you eat,
but always keep in mind that
seagulls subsist on garbage.

Forget the experience but never the lesson.

There is no more miserable
human being than one
who is indecisive.

210

If men knew what women do when they're alone, the engagement would be broken.

If you've been married
more than three times...
call in sick—or lease!

An optimist hasn't had much experience.

Experience is the name we give to our mistakes.

Spend major time with major people and casual time with casual people, because if you spend major time with casual people you become a casualty.